AF126404

BOOK ANALYSIS

By Corinne Herward

The Pursuit of Love

by Nancy Mitford

NANCY MITFORD

ENGLISH NOVELIST

- **Born in London in 1904.**
- **Died in Paris in 1973.**
- **Notable works:**
  - *Love in A Cold Climate* (1949), novel
  - *The Blessing* (1951), novel
  - *Don't Tell Alfred* (1960), novel

Born in 1904, Nancy Mitford was a glittering socialite whose life spanned the First and Second World Wars. One of six sisters, Mitford closely integrated her family life into her fiction. Although her pre-war novels, published in the 1930s, made little impression on the public, her later work caught the attention of the society it captured. Sharp, witty, and clever, Mitford's novels sketched the landed gentry with affection and nostalgia.

After Mitford's infatuation with the homosexual Hamish Erskine, she married Peter Rodd in 1933. Their marriage only lasted five years, and after its demise Mitford met and fell in love with Gaston Palewski. Inspired, Mitford published *The Pursuit of Love* in 1945, and subsequently moved to Paris in 1946. Mitford wrote *Love in a Cold Climate*, a sequel to *The Pursuit of Love*, in 1949, which received warm acclaim, and *Don't Tell Alfred*, a continuation of the series, in 1960. Mitford later became a columnist for *The Times* and wrote historical biographies of Madame de Pompadour (mistress to the French king Louis XV, 1721-1764) and Louis XIV (French king, 1638-1715) before illness overtook her. She died from Hodgkin's disease in 1973.

THE PURSUIT OF LOVE

A ROMANTIC SOCIAL COMEDY

- **Genre:** novel
- **Reference edition:** Mitford, N. (2010) *The Pursuit of Love*. London: Penguin.
- **1ˢᵗ edition:** 1945
- **Themes:** love, adolescence, maturity, inter-war years, society, wealth, aristocracy

Nancy Mitford's sparkling semi-autobiographical novel *The Pursuit of Love* was published in 1945. It received critical acclaim, its highly original tone and comedy setting it apart from Mitford's early work. The distinctive narration which blends the chatty girlhood voices of Fanny and Linda with the serious literary taste of Mitford herself creates an unusual blend of wit and reflection.

The Pursuit of Love begins by recounting the childhood adventures of Fanny and her cousins, the Radletts. From their relationship with their belligerent father, Fanny's Uncle Matthew, to their yearning to grow older and their attempts to learn about sex from animal husbandry manuals, the reader is plunged into the confusion of adolescence. Ultimately, *The Pursuit of Love* follows the beautiful Linda Radlett and her marriages to Tony Kroesig, a new-money banker, and the idealistic communist Christian Talbot. Finally, Linda finds love with Fabrice de Sauveterre – but it is not all she imagined it would be. Throughout *The Pursuit of Love* Mitford explores the privileged class of aristocracy that waned in the post-war era. Punctuated by wistful poignancy, Mitford is simultaneously idealistic and cautious about the pursuit of love and its ramifications.

SUMMARY

CHILDHOOD

The Pursuit of Love opens on the narrator, Fanny, visiting her cousins, the Radletts, at their family estate, Alconleigh. The fantastical and eccentric setting introduces a cast of unlikely yet charming characters; Uncle Matthew hosts child hunts where he chases the children over the estate, while Jassy Radlett hoards her money, waiting until she can escape to Hollywood. While the male Radletts are away at Eton, the girls hole up in the airing cupboard, the only warm place in the icy manor of Alconleigh. Here the Radletts host their secret society, 'the Hons', where they plot against the gamekeeper and discuss their many pets. Fanny tells us that the time she remembers best is the year she turned 14 and her guardian, Aunt Emily, got married to a man called Captain Warbeck, later affectionately referred to as Davy. Fanny's mother, we are told, is referred to as 'the Bolter', due to her habit of bolting from her husbands, and in Fanny's case, children. After Emily's marriage Fanny spends every holiday at Alconleigh with the Radletts.

Fanny is sent to boarding school, while the Radlett girls grow up without any education. As a result, Linda Radlett grows obsessed with her burgeoning romantic life, counting down the hours until her coming out party. The girls obsess over learning what sex is from a book about ducks, while they wonder what Oscar Wilde did to upset the grim and aggressive Uncle Matthew so much. Linda becomes depressed and bored while she waits for her life to begin. She counts down the hours by playing cards, and never develops any constructive pastimes or interests. Thus, Mitford begins her reflection on the dangers of raising girls without any other outlets than the pursuit of marriage and the goal of finding a husband.

MISMATCH

At last the fateful day arrives, and Linda and Fanny have a joint coming out party at Alconleigh. Lord Merlin, a family friend, decides to bring Tony Kroesig, a young and eligible banker, with him to the party to keep the gender balance even for dancing. "She took him, in short, for his own valuation," Fanny first explains Linda's attraction to the pompous Tony Kroesig (p. 52). Without any education or alternative experience, Linda falls for the first man she sees, and despite her family and friends' opposition, she marries Tony Kroesig. This is the beginning of a short and miserable marriage for Linda. "The young man she had fallen in love with [...] melted away upon further acquaintance, and proved to have been a chimera, never to have existed outside her imagination" (p. 88). Mitford points out the lack of tradition and different customs that make Linda an outsider in her husband's middle-class family, from their houses to their spending habits. Meanwhile Linda's child, Moira, disgusts her mother, and spends more time with her grandparents than with Linda.

While Linda is visiting Moira at her grandparents, she meets the handsome and radical young communist Christian Talbot. Christian is immediately transfixed by Linda, and she is charmed by the bad manners he directs towards the Kroesigs. Mitford again describes Linda as "a plum that was ripe for the shaking," due to her disinterest in her child, her failing marriage and lack of profession (p. 98). Linda falls head over heels in love with Christian Talbot and runs away to Perpignan to work in a refugee camp. Linda again grows miserable under the strain of Christian's disinterest. At last, seeing how absorbed Christian is in communism and the martyr-like Lavender Davis, Linda once again runs away, this time to Paris. Turned away at the train station due to an expired ticket, Linda sinks in despair, and cries while she sits on her suitcase and wonders what to do.

TRUE LOVE

While Linda is sobbing on her suitcase, an attractive Frenchman nearby sits down and begins to laugh at her. Linda allows this man to lead her to a nearby hotel, where he explains that his name is Fabrice de Sauveterre, that he is a wealthy duke, and that he intends to have an affair with Linda. Disconcerted, Linda allows herself to be put up in a hotel and stays with Fabrice until the outbreak of the Second World War. The two begin an affair that grows to love, and Linda becomes much happier, at last having found what she was looking for. Linda returns to London in 1939 to escape the violence in Europe. Fabrice visits her briefly and admits that he loves her but could never bring himself to repeat the phrases he used in his long years of womanising. In London, Linda discovers that Tony, now married to his former mistress, is planning to flee the war and go to America. Linda regards this as extremely unpatriotic and insists on being allowed to see Moira before she leaves. Tony assents, but on Moira's assertion that she would be too frightened of air raids to stay in London, Linda gives up on her daughter in disgust. She explains to Fanny that she could never allow herself to have any affection for her daughter, because it would have chained her to the Kroesigs forever. Alone in her London townhouse, Fanny discovers Linda after a particularly bad night of bombing and realises that Linda is heavily pregnant. Fanny persuades Linda to return to Alconleigh, where Louisa, Fanny's mother the Bolter, her boyfriend Juan, Emily and Davy are all now living. The war drags on and as Alconleigh emerges unscathed into spring, Louisa gives birth. This is shortly followed by Fanny and Linda who go into labour on the same day. However, Linda dies in childbirth, and a heartbroken Fanny adopts her son. Fabrice dies at the same time as Linda, shot by the Gestapo for participating in the French resistance. While Fanny is still in the nursing home that Linda died in, the Bolter calls to visit her, and suggests that it is better for Linda to have died, rather than to discover she had been fooled in love once again.

CHARACTER STUDY

LINDA RADLETT

The protagonist of *The Pursuit of Love*, Linda Radlett leads an exciting, if not particularly happy life. Her vivacious, joyful personality shines through the text, and Linda is adored by her family and friends, though not by her two husbands. In the words of Fanny, "Linda distilled, mentally and physically, the very essence of the Radlett family [...] There was something furious about her, even when she laughed, which she did a great deal, and always as if forced to against her will" (p. 12). Linda is beautiful, witty, and fun. Yet many characters misunderstand Linda or think that she is vapid and frivolous, and even Fanny accuses Linda of wasting her youth on frippery.

After her aimless childhood, brought up without any pursuits apart from occasional hunting outings, Linda becomes obsessed with the promise of romance, and leaps headfirst into marriage with an uninspiring banker named Tony

Kroesig. She is soon liberated from her illusions and realises that the man she married does not laugh easily, never indulges in romantic gestures, is not dashing, and generally is not the man she thought she was going to be married to. When Linda's child, Moira, is born, Linda refuses to have anything to do with her and rejects her from her first moment. Inevitably, Linda leaves her family and enters a second marriage with Christian Talbot, an ardent communist. Linda realises that Christian does not love her either, and she flees to Paris in despair.

While in Paris, Linda meets an exciting stranger named Fabrice, and in a dizzyingly short space of time the pair begin an affair that stretches until the beginning of the Second World War when Linda returns to London for safety. Linda becomes pregnant with Fabrice's child while he is visiting London and refuses to move from her bomb-stricken apartment until it is reduced to rubble, whereupon she returns to Alconleigh. While at Alconleigh Linda returns to an adolescent state, where she lolls about in the airing cupboard as she did when she was a teenager, and begins counting down the hours, just as she did when she was waiting for the love of her life to arrive. However, Linda dies in childbirth and never sees Fabrice again. Whether or not the two would have had a long and happy life is left ambiguous, leaving Linda's character growth as an unanswerable question.

FANNY LOGAN

Mitford's narrator provides a contrast to the exciting Linda. Fanny is the only child of a woman called 'the Bolter' for her habit of leaving her husbands, while her mysterious father has a series of flings with women all over the age of 40, leaving Fanny as the sole heir of £15 000 a year – a small fortune in the 1930s. When the book begins, Fanny is under the guardianship of her mother's sister, Aunt Emily, her main guardian, but also her mother's other sister Aunt Sadie, who is married to Uncle Matthew and is the mother of the Radlett children.

When Aunt Emily gets married to Captain Warbeck, Fanny spends more time at Alconleigh, the Radlett family estate. She grows closer to her cousin Linda and becomes a part of the family despite Uncle Matthew disliking her natural timidity and the habits she has picked up at boarding school, where, he says, she has lost "every ounce of feminine charm" (p. 12).

Fanny's narration does not deal with the infinitesimal realistic details of Linda's life; rather she paints broad strokes, sketching out Linda's life with the passion she lived it. In contrast, Fanny's life is punctuated by the humdrum squabbles that characterise any family life: meals, nurses, illnesses. Linda tells Fanny not to pity her, as she has had 11 months of perfect happiness with Fabrice, and after all, not everyone gets that. In the later part of the novel, Fanny is increasingly preoccupied by the comparisons between her mother and Linda, as she tries to discern the truth in an uncertain time.

UNCLE MATTHEW

The eccentric and erratic Uncle Matthew is our introduction to life at Alconleigh, as one of the first images of the book is the framed entrenching tool with which he beat eight Germans to death during World War I. Uncle Matthew is a complex individual, and despite his gruff exterior he has a soft spot for Linda, who is his favourite child.

Uncle Matthew cries despondently though Linda's wedding ceremony; yet he never visits her in London, even during the air raids. He is a staunch yet sentimental figure who while in the House of Lords votes for blood sports and steel traps yet votes against exporting old horses to Belgium. Uncle Matthew is also notable for his denunciation of girls' boarding schools, as in early chapters he claims that they are the destruction of feminine charms, and while, Fanny claims, Uncle Matthew is not against his daughters having an education, he dislikes the middle-class existence that they imprint onto their students. Uncle Matthew is a symbol of pre-war England, and although his conservative views often conflict with the explosive relationships of Linda, Jassy and the Bolter, the family remain close.

LOUISA RADLETT

The dullest member of the Radlett family, Louisa stands in opposition to Linda in every respect. Her coming out party is a disastrous collection of elderly gentlemen from the House of Lords, and she represents a prosaic ordinariness that is bleak in contrast to the vivid life that Mitford paints through Linda. Almost immediately after her coming out party, Louisa marries a Scottish peer, Sir John Fort William, who is 20 years her elder. After moving away and having several children, Louisa is utterly forgotten by everyone through the plain monogamous life she leads. However, with the advent of the Second World War Louisa's house is occupied by the army and she moves back to Alconleigh to be safe. "What do we get for sticking by our dull old husbands year after year?" (p. 154) Louisa complains, envying Linda's sables. Although Louisa is bored, she never rebels against the plain life she leads and carries on year after year in her career of motherhood and marriage.

TONY KROESIG

Tony, the unromantic new money banker who marries Linda, is at once dashing and unremarkable. Linda first meets Tony at her coming out party, when Lord Merlin includes him as a late addition to the party. "What could possibly have induced Linda to marry Anthony Kroesig?" Fanny asks the reader, before explaining that

it was simply that she was in love with him
(p. 54). Fanny lists Tony's myriad attractions:
he is in his last year at Oxford, he is a member
of Bullingdon, he has a Rolls-Royce, beautiful
horses, fashionable clothes and luxurious rooms
and he entertains in style. Tony is tall and fair
and pompous, and his confidence in himself
tricks Linda into believing that he is as grand as
he believes. However, Linda's naivete leads her
to overlook the fact that Tony's good spirits are
induced by alcohol when they first meet, and his
early ardency fades into dour disinterest when
they are married. Although Linda is known for
her virtue, Tony keeps a mistress named Pixie
Townsend, whom he later marries, and they
eventually flee to America together to escape
the war.

CHRISTIAN TALBOT

Christian Talbot is an extraordinarily handsome
upper-class socialist, whose father is friends
with the Kroesigs. His complete disinterest in
money is a charming contrast with the obsessive
ardour with which the Kroesig family regard
profit. Christian's radical communism, combined

with Linda's utter despair, induce Linda to run away from Tony with Christian. He insists on marrying her, despite Linda's protestations, and they are married in a courthouse. Linda moves into a small flat where she learns how to do housework for the first time. However, Christian is unable to relate to Linda on a personal level, as she herself states "he only cares for ideas" (p. 102) and hardly notices whether Linda is there or not. However, in pursuing Christian's ideals, Linda loses her sense of self. While working in a refugee camp, Linda comes to realise how reliant her second husband is on the practical yet dismal Lavender Davis and resolves to leave him to her. Linda hardly ever wastes another thought on Christian, although we are told that he willingly allows Fanny to adopt Fabrice's child, despite being the legal father.

FABRICE DE SAUVETERRE

The man that Linda finally finds love with is an enigma in the text. A womanising, almost mythical figure of the French resistance, Fabrice finds Linda when she is at the lowest ebb of her life. He picks her up from the train station, and she is almost instantly attracted to him and his complete composure. Fabrice is an extremely wealthy Duke who installs Linda in an apartment, where he keeps her in clothes and flowers. It is at this point that Fanny says that Linda is feeding upon "a diet of honey-dew" (p. 154). While the couple live in Paris, Fabrice often puts up barriers with Linda, refusing to indulge in romantic phrases. Later, when he visits her in London, Fabrice confesses that he loves Linda, and that it was this love that prevented him from trotting out the well-worn phrases that he had used with many other women. Fabrice leaves London, and although Linda receives a mysterious cryptic letter from him, there is no other communication between the pair. Linda dies without ever telling Fabrice that she is pregnant, and Fanny tells us that Fabrice dies at the same time, shot by the Gestapo for his role in the war.

THE BOLTER

Fanny's mother is one of the most significant characters in *The Pursuit of Love*. Although she is only briefly mentioned in the beginning of the book, the Bolter appears to have left a long and unhappy string of men behind her. Fanny writes that although Aunt Emily and Davy were very clever to turn her mother into a family joke rather than an enduring disgrace, it is clear that the pockmarked history of her mother's life has been derided in and out of social circles. The Bolter returns in the final chapters of *The Pursuit of Love*, having crossed the Swiss Alps to escape World War II with her unintelligible Spanish companion, Juan. Ultimately, the Bolter suggests that it is better for Linda to be dead rather than to have led a life like hers. Mitford ends *The Pursuit of Love* with the Bolter's rebuttal to Fanny's defence of Linda, saying that one always thinks they have met the love of their life when they run away with someone.

ANALYSIS

NARRATIVE VOICE

Fanny Logan has two voices in *The Pursuit of Love*: the younger Fanny, who does not always understand everything that is going on around her, and the older and worldlier Fanny, who is fully aware of people's characters, their flaws and their mistakes. Zoë Heller argues that the strength of Nancy Mitford's first successful novel lies in the creation of a narrative voice which is at once girlish and charming yet yearns with a nostalgia that often lends itself to poignancy regarding the tragedy of the book (Heller, 2010). This can be seen in the opening paragraph, when Fanny reflects on the photograph of Aunt Sadie and her children at Alconleigh: "There they are, held like flies, in the amber of that moment [...] the decades taking them further and further from that happiness and promise of youth" (p. 1). Fanny admits that Linda was not only her favourite cousin, but for many years her favourite person. At the beginning of the book, the reader assumes that a husband has superseded Linda in Fanny's affections, exacerbating the wrench we feel with the narrator when Linda dies. While sentimental, Fanny's voice shares the same cutting acerbity that Mitford displayed in her letters to her sisters, and she penetrates to the core of the comparisons between the Bolter and Linda herself. Although Fanny never blames Linda for abandoning Moira, the comparisons between the two are undeniable and in the final chapters of the book Fanny throws the Bolter and Linda into the same light repeatedly. Eventually we understand that although Fanny insists that *The Pursuit of Love* is Linda's story, it reflects on her own journey with her mother, her childhood and her abandonment. This voice with its elusive preoccupation shows that the perspective in *The Pursuit of Love* is often biased and reveals a character deeply interested in her own concerns in the last pages of the novel. Careful readers may grow to wonder if *The Pursuit of Love* is really Linda's story at all. Like Linda, Nancy Mitford was a member of an infamous family, and this experience is examined in *The Pursuit of Love*. Mitford grew accustomed to reading about her sisters' behaviour in newspapers and borrowed from their lives for her work. When the reader contrasts this compilation of experience and personality with the blended characters of the Bolter and Linda, the questions that Mitford, perhaps unconsciously, raises about family, self, reputation and representation shine through this seemingly light-hearted novel.

LOVE – ACTUALLY?

One of the most pertinent questions that the reader has after finishing *The Pursuit of Love* is whether Fabrice and Linda would have remained together if they had not died. It is a question that cannot be answered, yet the Bolter's mournful speech at the close of the book suggests that they would not have. Certainly, Fanny believes that they would have, but she speaks regretfully at the close of Linda's life. The reader is left to wonder if they would have passed out of each other's lives at the close of five years as Fabrice promised, leaving Fanny to play Aunt Emily to Linda's son. Linda believes that she is in love three times throughout *The Pursuit of Love*. The dawn of Fanny and Linda's adolescence begins with Aunt Emily's marriage to Davy, and from that moment the girls yearn to be in love. Linda immediately falls under Tony Kroesig's spell the first time she lays eyes on him, and is deaf to the warnings of her friends and family. Then, just as suddenly, Linda leaves Tony for Christian Talbot and becomes an embarrassment to her family by espousing communism at the dining tables of aristocratic families, with Fanny describing her as follows:

> "Linda was a plum ripe for the shaking [...] Intelligent and energetic, but with no outlet for her energies, unhappy in her marriage, uninterested in her child, and inwardly oppressed with a sense of futility, she was in the mood to take up some cause, or to embark upon a love affair." (p. 98)

It was not because she was in love that she married, Mitford makes abundantly clear, but due to the external circumstances that shaped marriage into the only pursuit of her life. Love, true love, that cannot be mistaken for the passing fancy of Tony and Christian, finds Linda when she is not in pursuit, casting the title in an ironic light. And yet Fabrice's devotion can be called into question, when Linda hears that he has been calling other women for hours at a time. Even the finality of Linda's love is undercut as the Bolter says that "One always thinks that [they have found the love of their life]. Every, every time" (p. 204).

NOTHING IS SACRED

One of the most notable features of Mitford's writing style is the sharp and witty banter that the characters engage in with one another. While their inconsequential tone quashes the magnitude of their remarks, Mitford often touches on tragedies through her trademark humour. "It's rather sad," Linda says, "to belong, as we do, to a lost generation [...] We might just as well never have lived at all, I do think it's a shame" (p. 84). Some critics have argued that Mitford's manner of laughing at and dodging the turmoil of the 20th century denotes immorality and irresponsibility. Yet the personal impact of history is an issue that is clearly raised throughout *The Pursuit of Love*. While Mitford does indulge in light and sparkling chatter through her novels, it only highlights the gut-wrenching sadness of the opening and close of her novel. If the 20th century is, as the historian Eric Hobsbawm has suggested, "an age of extremes", then Mitford's novel takes these extremes and warps them humorously. When Linda is pressed to describe her radical communist husband, she says flippantly, "He's a frightfully serious man, you know, a Communist, and so am I now, and we are surrounded by comrades all day, and they are terrific Hons, and there's an anarchist" (p. 95). Mitford slyly pokes fun at the violent ideals that characterised the era, and the family that she was born into. Mitford also takes the same tone regarding the sanctity of marriage, walking her characters through the laughable double standards of her day. Linda is divorced by Tony when she goes to live with Christian, but Linda reveals to Fanny that she knows Tony will be relieved that he is now free to marry his mistress, which he does. The Bolter, with her succession of marriages, and Fanny's father with his string of older women, set the tone for the irrepressible glee with which Mitford splits apart the nuclear family. Aunt Sadie, with her forgetfulness, worn out by childbirth, and Louisa, who contemptuously remarks upon her "dull old husband" (p. 154), are our examples of happy marriage. Even the narrator claims that she and her husband are only as happy as married people can be. Perhaps, Mitford suggests, it is the pursuit of love that is the sweetest, and not the daily monotony of its consummation. Mitford's refusal to darken her tone with the social calamities of her day allows *The Pursuit of Love* to retain a breezy attitude and encourages the reader to laugh at human foibles.

FURTHER REFLECTION

SOME QUESTIONS TO THINK ABOUT...

- One of the jokes in *The Pursuit of Love* is Fanny's mother, referred to as 'the Bolter' by the other characters. Is the Bolter a funny character or a sad one? Make a case for and against Mitford's use of her for comedy.
- Why does Linda choose Tony, and then Christian to marry? Are her choices based on their characteristics or on hers?
- Mitford is known for having painted a portrait of society in the inter-war years through *The Pursuit of Love*. How does our modern view of love and marriage contrast with hers?
- Fanny admits at the beginning of the novel that Linda was her favourite cousin, and her favourite human. Do you think Fanny is a reliable narrator?
- "The lives of women like Linda and me are not so much fun when one begins to grow older," the Bolter says to Fanny (p. 204). Does Mitford

undermine Fabrice and Linda's love story by comparing Linda to the Bolter?

- Andrew O'Hagan has referred to Mitford's style as "the posh aesthetic" and denounces Mitford's wit by claiming that there is a moral vacuity in *The Pursuit of Love* (O'Hagan, 2007). Do you agree with O'Hagan's claims? Why or why not?

- At the beginning of the novel Fanny writes about a photograph of the Radletts sitting around a tea table, where she claims, "the minutes, the days the years taking them further and further from that happiness and promise of youth, from the [...] dreams they dreamed for themselves" (p. 1). Fanny often bemoans that Linda had no tangible profit from her experiences and that she had nothing to show for it. Do you think Linda's life was empty?

- Linda refuses to love or know her daughter Moira because she does not want to keep a link to the Kroesig family. Is it wrong of Linda to reject her daughter this way? Why or why not?

We want to hear from you!
Leave a comment on your online library
and share your favourite books on social media!

FURTHER READING

REFERENCE EDITION

- Mitford, N. (2010) *The Pursuit of Love*. London: Penguin.

REFERENCE STUDIES

- O'Hagan, A. (2007) Poor Hitler. *London Review of Books*. [Online]. [Accessed 4 February 2019]. 29(22), pp. 24-25. Available from: <https://www.lrb.co.uk/v29/n22/andrew-ohagan/poor-hitler>

- Heller, Z. (2010) Zoë Heller on Nancy Mitford. *The Telegraph*. [Online]. [Accessed 18 January 2019]. Available from: <https://www.telegraph.co.uk/culture/books/7398341/Zoe-Heller-on-Nancy-Mitford.html>

- Hobsbawm, E. (1996) *The Age of Extremes*. London: Vintage Books.

- (No date) Nancy Mitford. *Wikipedia*. [Online]. [Accessed 15 January 2019]. Available from: <https://en.wikipedia.org/wiki/Nancy_Mitford>

- (No date) The Pursuit of Love. *Wikipedia*. [Online]. [Accessed 14 January 2019]. Available from: <https://en.wikipedia.org/wiki/The_Pursuit_of_Love>

ADDITIONAL SOURCES

- Hepburn, A. (1999) The Fate of the Modern Mistress: Nancy Mitford and The Comedy of Marriage. *MFS Modern Fiction Studies*. 45(2), pp. 340-368.

- Mitford, N. (2011) *The Penguin Complete Novels of Nancy Mitford*. London: Penguin.

- Mosley, C. ed. (2008) *The Mitfords: Letters between Six Sisters*. New York: Harper Perennial.

- Thompson, L. (2004) *Life in a Cold Climate: Nancy Mitford the Biography*. New York: Headline Book Publishing.

- Thompson, L. (2001) *Take Six Girls: The Lives of The Mitford Sisters*. New York: Head of Zeus.

ADAPTATIONS

- *Love in a Cold Climate.* (2001) [TV Series]. Tom Cooper Dir. UK: BBC.

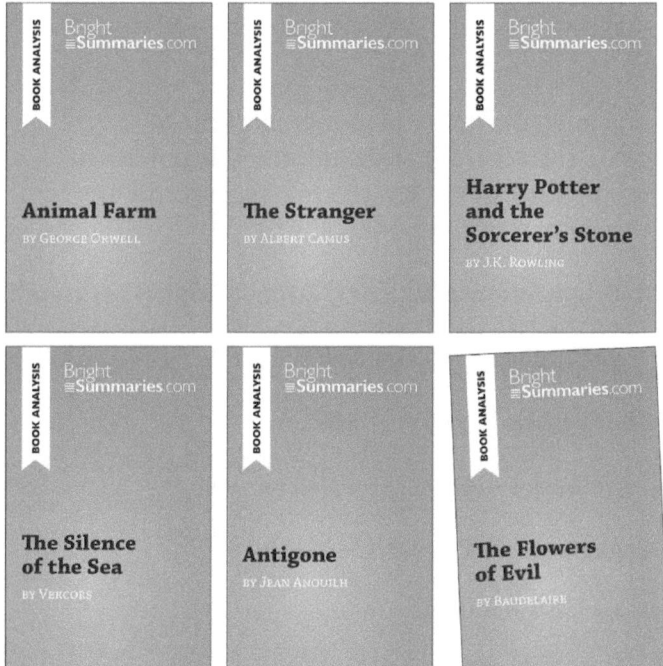

www.brightsummaries.com

Ebook EAN: 9782808017589

Paperback EAN: 9782808017596

Legal Deposit: D/2019/12603/46

Cover: © Primento

Digital conception by Primento, the digital partner of
publishers.